Copyright 2021 © by Leslie A. Piggott
Published December 2021
Published by Indies United Publishing House, LLC

Cover art & interior artwork by Leslie A. Piggott

All rights reserved worldwide. No part of this publication may be replicated, redistributed, or given away in any form without the prior written consent of the author/publisher or the terms relayed to you herein.

ISBN: 978-1-64456-393-9 (paperback)
ISBN: 978-1-64456-395-3 (ePub)
ISBN: 978-1-64456-394-6 (Mobi)

Library of Congress Control Number: 2021948477

INDIES UNITED PUBLISHING HOUSE, LLC
P.O. BOX 3071
QUINCY, IL 62305-3071

www.indiesunited.net

Dedication

To Brad: thank you for being my best friend and my biggest fan
To Abby and Simon: thank you for being the two best kids ever

Thank you to all of my friends and family who read these poems and gave me feedback along the way. You are a treasure to me.

One big shout out to Lisa and the gang with Indies United: None of this would be possible without you!

Table of Contents

Emerging Hope..2
In Just a Year..4
Reset..8
Rising..11
Staring at the Edge of the End..14
Level Up..17
Kind..19
Joy of Tomorrow..21
Melody..23
Anticipation..25
Pain Revisited..28
Two New Roads..30
Compassion of Life..32
Infinite Circle..35
Neighbor..36
Struggling..39
Dear 2021..42
Weary..45
Of Celebration..48
Begging..51
Community..53
Power of God..54
Perceiving Joy..56
Power of One..58
Rest..60
Escape..62

Awash with Emotion..64

Light..66

Storms..68

Endless..70

Art in Words

Written and Illustrated by Leslie A. Piggott

Emerging Hope

Day after day
Month after month
Watching the case numbers
Trending up and down
Like a terrifying rollercoaster
That seems to never stop,
Let alone allow you to exit.
News of a vaccine
Lifts our hopes.
The glacial-pace of the rollout
Sends them crashing back down.
The duality of these two rides
Exhausts me.
Yet God is faithful.
I am undeserving,
Low-priority on the list,
Yet God heard.
God saw.
God answered.
Silent tears of joy
Pour from my heart.
Hope is restored.

In Just a Year

One year has passed
One year since things changed
In a heartbeat
Have we changed?
As we watched our world morph
From one where we couldn't be closer
To one where we had to stay apart,
Did we not adapt?
Physically, our interactions could not continue.
Still, we found ways to be together.
We began to learn what was safe,
And what must be restricted.
Our changed world brought light to disparities.
We had to face inequalities
We had once ignored.
Opportunities to unite
Or further divide
Surfaced.
We spoke of working together.
Of listening more.
We found ways to celebrate:

Weddings, births, graduation parades, birthday parades, promotions.
We suffered losses:
Loss of income
Loss of business
Loss of togetherness
Loss of life, of loved ones.
Even grief was touched
By the changes of our world.
Forced to minimize,
Compartmentalize,
And delay
Overwhelming feelings.
We became more creative:
Baking
Building
Painting
Gardening
Writing
Singing.
We took new classes
And learned new skills.
But what did we learn in the silence?
Did we learn to look
For the good in our neighbor,

Instead of expecting the worst?
Did we learn to see
The light in the darkness,
In the shadows that continued
To fall within our lives?
Did we learn to love
More fully?
Did we learn to accept
Our neighbor,
To accept their love?
Did we experience kindness
And show kindness in return?
Have we realized that we can?
That in generosity, we will find abundance.

Reset

Through struggles, hardships, and losses,
Our questions and doubts
Pouring into endless voids.
The once-hard exterior of our past
Crinkling like trees in winter.
As pieces of long-held "truths" chip
From the life we knew,
We seek to discover
How we went wrong.
We view this new vulnerable life as broken,
Yearning to reform the shell that once gave us security,
Yet wanting to grow from what we are trying to learn.
Wanting to find a better version of ourselves
Within the pieces of our past that we desperately cling to.
We pray for guidance
Asking for forgiveness.
We've been gifted time.
Time to reset
Time to unlearn our life biases.
Time to step back and stop hating.
Time to step forward and offer love.
Can we, through our brokenness,

See the pain that others endure?
Can we rectify our missteps?
We long to feel whole again—
To feel hope again.
Like a windy road, life continues to turn.
We look for light around each bend,
Wondering what crisis might strike next.
Yet we must persevere,
We must not quit.
The Light is not gone.
It is within each of us.
By joining together, we can make our world a brighter place.

Rising

The fragility of life
Within the past year
Has remained in the foreground.
Every event
Every milestone
Every moment
Accented
By the pandemic.
Every experience has been viewed
Through the lens
Of precaution
Of protection
Of... pandemic.
A year full of asterisks.
Last year,
We approached Easter
In disbelief.
We could not gather
Each day brought new fears,
New cancellations.
We celebrated on screens
Wondered how many more

WEEKS
We would be apart.
This year feels different.
We've found ways to be together.
As the sun sets on Saturday,
We anticipate Sunday morning,
It's not only the joy of Easter Sunday,
It's the hope we can see in tomorrow.
We've endured more than we could imagine.
We've persevered through enumerable crises.
The pandemic isn't over.
But unlike last year,
When we stared at the face of uncertainty,
This year
Our hope is rising with the Son.

Staring at the Edge of the End

Lately, it feels like we're staring at the edge of "The End"
Trying to imagine what it's like on the other side.
Like a mom window shopping at Christmas,
We wonder what experiences we'll find on the other side of the glass.
We have yearned for restoration,
For renewal.
We celebrate each shot
As one step closer.
We still do not know how many steps remain.
We can now almost imagine
A day when the words,
"Back during the pandemic..."
Are spoken with regularity.
But what will those days look like?
Will we hug, shake hands?
Some days, we trudge along,
Feeling that we are no closer to "The End" than yesterday.
Other days, we find hope,
Feel our pace quicken,
Think the light at the end of the proverbial tunnel is growing brighter.

And we stare into the distance
Wondering what it's like on the other side.

Level Up

We have reached a new level
A new balancing act in the pandemic.
Behind us are the days of constant checking, refreshing,
For our turn
Our shot.
Now we hope that hesitancy can be overcome.
How do we unpoliticize science?

Kind

We say that we care.
That we are kind.
"Kind-ness over right-ness."
We can protect each other,
But we are stubborn.
We have become so polarized
That we can't hear our neighbor.
We can't offer empathy
When we won't stop to listen to the hurting.
We have forgotten who our neighbor is.
We have stopped trying to love them.
We must reconnect,
Cross the line we drew in the sand.
Come together, united.
Come together and love.

Joy of Tomorrow

Sometimes,
We can't see joy through the haze of pain.
Sometimes,
We are called to be the light
That shines through someone else's pain.
Lately, it feels like each day brings new suffering.
Will we always be waiting on tomorrow's joy?
Have we become so dulled by present struggles,
That we cannot experience today's joys?
The race against disease and towards healing
Is weighing heavy.
Maybe no longer on the forefront,
Yet constantly in the back of our minds.
When does relief come?
Glimpses of normalcy bring hope,
While surges worldwide deliver more fear.
Where do we find joy today?
When will we see a finish line?

Melody

When the melody of your heart slows,
Beats
With great effort,
When no breath feels sufficient,
When your emotions make you weary
And try to break you—
You are not alone.
You are held.
Take time to heal,
To find restoration.
Your melody is not lost,
It will sing again.

Anticipation

Months of preparation
Not knowing if it would come to fruition.
Like a plane in a holding pattern
Waiting for a storm to lessen
Hoping for clearance
For an opportunity.
I have rested and refueled
Chasing a dream
That seems to be continually out of reach.
Then I lost the chance to keep trying.
Amid repeated cancellations
And postponements
I have tried to persevere
Tried to hold space for my goal,
To not abandon it in frustration.
Now just days away
From the starting line
The adrenaline from this anticipation,
Like overwhelming joy,
Is a rush.
No matter the outcome
It will feel like a victory.

I will still strive to make my mark
Never again taking for granted
That next race.

Pain Revisited

Experiencing the judgment of one's character
Leaves a wound within your soul.
A wound that easily reopens
Upon pain revisited.
Words that tear you down
Looks that bring you shame.
The ache of seeing one you love
Struck down
Degraded.
Where does relief come?
How do you heal?
What makes you whole?
God, in you we have all things.
How do I resolve this pain?
How do I let go of the control it has?
Is it perfection I seek?
God, show me the path forward.
Grant me peace.

Two New Roads

The famous words
"Two roads diverged into a wood…"
Teaching their readers to be bold and unique.
And while I celebrate individuality,
At least one occasion arises
When I hope the common path
Is the better choice.
When choosing a response,
You can choose to be right,
Or you can choose to be kind.
Let's make KIND
Be the well-traveled path.

Compassion of Life

Feeling heartbroken
Like a child
Crying on a merry-go-round that won't stop
The pandemic refusing to relinquish its hold on the world
Breakthrough cases
Delta variant
Exponential growth
Words that I am tired of hearing.
How did we get here?
Again.
Why is this still the life we live?
When will we agree to work together?
Hope after hope
Repeatedly dashed
By an infection.
People refusing to hear the truth
Crying hoax
Declaring false news.
Daily prayers,
Pleas, that God will soften hearts
That distrust and paranoia can be overcome.
That 'we over me' will rule the day.

May we hear our neighbor
When they fear or hurt
Meet our neighbor
Where they stand
Love our neighbor
Amidst our continued differences.

Infinite Circle

Life feels like it's stuck in an infinite circle
Of a knitted sweater.
One small twist in the fibers
And you're right back where you started.
We step back
Reassess
Yet cannot find the exit.
I pray for resolution
For wisdom
For unity.
Have we lost our footing?
Dropped a stitch?
I am yearning for answers
For relief
Like a pendulum
It seems we swing without gaining.
We fight the same battles.
My heart cries out
And holds fast to God's comfort.

Neighbor

Who is my neighbor?
The famous question
Raised to the timeless Teacher.
We know the story,
But today we still ask the question.
What does my neighbor look like?
Surely, not different from me.
What does my neighbor think?
Surely, exactly what I think.
What does my neighbor wear?
Surely, the styles that I choose.
How does my neighbor vote?
Surely, the same way I vote.
What does my neighbor believe?
Surely, the things that I believe.
How could my neighbor be hurting,
When I am not hurting?
How could my neighbor be scared,
When I am not scared?
When did I define neighbor by looking in the mirror?
Community is created in differences.
Community is richer with variety.

We are all God's children.
Let us all be neighbors.

Struggling

The pain of reality
Is cutting me down.
Each day
A portion of my hopefulness
Is raw and weakened.
I wonder how it heals.
Is it scarred,
Free of the elasticity
That once bounced a smile to my face?
How much more?
How much longer?
Have we grown callous
Or deaf to the suffering?
I don't know what I miss
Or what I'm longing for.
I feel hurt reading the anger
In other people's words.
The chasm of our differences
Grows by the day.
It's "us versus them"
But who is "us"
And who is "them"?

God, hear my prayer.
My heart is aching.
The salves of yesterday
No longer soothe.
I know You're here.
I need relief.

Dear 2021

Dear 2021,
I see you.
You stood near the horizon
Dressed as hope.
You crashed into our lives.
Promised resolution and unification.
We felt hopeful
For the first time in months.
We thought we could see the last hurdle
Before the finish line.
But 2021—
You fooled us.
It was just the start of another lap.
I have tripped over barriers,
I have cleared others.
I have fallen down,
A bit broken.
You have brought me to tears,
But I will not stay down.
I will persevere.
You have masqueraded as hope,
But you will not steal mine.

"For these three remain,
Faith,
Hope, and
Love."

Weary

O Lord,
I am weary.
Mentally exhausted.
Emotionally drained.
Does relief come if I quit caring?
Can I quit caring?
Is this fatigue ubiquitous
Throughout my community?
I once thought we stood
At the edge of the end.
Now I wonder
If that end exists.
I can find no escape—
No Emergency Shut Off button.
We are entangled by the vine of the pandemic.
Like the kudzu,
It blocks our ability to thrive,
Pulls us back into the quicksand.
We have struggled
Endured
Continually wrestling, seeking freedom.
The vine keeps us ensnared,

Mercilessly, it holds us captive.
Please, God, Please.
Help us find relief.

Of Celebration

Celebrating
In the midst of crisis
Of crises, even.
The world
Somehow growing more uncertain
By the day.
Yet life continues.
Graduations
Weddings
Births.
The ceremony of life proceeds, undaunted.
We struggle with the why—
Why is there so much suffering?
Why is there so much hate?
Why can't everyone just get along?
We stand amongst these trials,
We are offered small windows of celebration,
Brief respites of peace,
Chance opportunities to escape.
Hearing our children laugh,
Celebrating milestones,
Living life

Even when it is hard.
We walk through it together,
Stumbling upon moments of joy,
Sometimes when we least expect it.

Begging

Here I sit
As close to begging as I get
Please
Hear my cry
Send protection
We feel so vulnerable
Help us
Free us from this anxiety
We are broken down
Our stores are depleted
We want to hope
But the pain—the angst—
Is so heavy
We are persevering
We are trying
It feels like we are losing
Please send relief
We are running on fumes.

Community

Trusting

Hoping

Seeking

Yet feeling abandoned.

We stood together

Though apart

We exercised precaution

And showed restraint.

We are all weary,

Yes, we are fatigued.

People say

Our children are our future

But no longer seem to care.

We speak of our rights

Of our freedoms

But have lost that space we held

For the youngest members of society.

Are we "a unified body of individuals"?

If one suffers,

We all suffer.

It seems like callous disregard.

It hurts.

It feels like community, broken.

Power of God

Creator God,
Who am I to question your wisdom,
To ask if your judgment is right.
Your creation:
Awe-inspiring.
Countless times
You have moved in our lives
Shown compassion
Given comfort
Healed the broken
And met all needs.
Our world is hurting,
Creation sighs again
With groans too deep for words.
How many times do we fight this battle?
How long will the suffering last?
I know that you hear me.
I know you are with us.
You see my exhaustion.
You haven't deserted me.
Please, help us end what plagues us.

Perceiving Joy

Continually longing for what's been lost
Struggling to anticipate what once was fun
An undercurrent of uncertainty
Constantly ripping the sparkle from life.
What has become of normal?
Floundering
Searching for purchase
Pausing
Breathing
Observing
Choosing to find joy
Daily.
Picking up my yellow pen
Seeing the sunshine in the words.
Joy is still present.
It is not lost.

Power of One

Consider yourself.
You are but one.
Insignificant?
Maybe.
Motivated?
Hopefully.
Can one person precipitate change?
Whose example do you follow?
Who follows yours?
A circle of influence.
You perform unknowingly.
Observed by an unseen audience.
Insignificant?
Hardly.

Rest

Constantly working
Striving for perfection
Hearing I am enough
But not accepting it
Seeking to be unblemished
Without blame
Overwhelmed with shame
At any perceived misstep
Fighting to climb the mountaintop
To be free of disqualifications
To be my best self
Bypassing moments of rest
In effort to be more
Desiring the title of success
Hearing again a voice to be still
To yield my endless work
"Cast off this burdensome yoke—
Find rest, O weary one.
You are loved,
You are enough."

Escape

Imagining

A carefree space

Weightless

Soaring

Unencumbered

By today's uncertainties

Yesterday's fears

Tomorrow's hopes

Anything is possible

Limitless

Acceptance and love are abundant

Are the norm

Life

Fully lived

Abounding with joy

May it be more

Than mere figment.

Awash with Emotion

Many have gone before

Have suffered, struggled, yearned

For relief

My emotions

Often swelling to spilling over

How possibly could one match this?

Trudging along

Trying not to drain my empathy bucket

Compassion fatigue

Overwhelms our caregivers

The flood of emotions

Trickle to a drought

There is no pain with indifference,

But also no joy.

We pray for renewal

And hope for relief.

Light

Each of us

Possess an inner beauty

A light

We see it shine

When we feel loved

When we know we are valued

This light

Can be shared

Magnified

Broadened

As we recognize

Respect, even

Our neighbor

We can be a light in the darkness

We can love.

Storms

Navigating a new surge
Much like the ones before it
How easily I forget
How quickly I feel panicked
We will have trials
It will not be easy
But we will not be lost
Nor forgotten
No storm lasts forever.

Endless

How many ways can you say "I'm breaking"?
How many times?
Overcoming battles and trials
Thinking you've reached the summit
While another peak looms in the distance.
Is there a Google search that tells you when this ends?
Drawing again, against hope
Repeatedly stymied by setbacks and outbreaks
Days overlapping into weeks...months...a year
Still we must wait
Cling to hope
A new day is coming
Working together
We will see it.

www.ingramcontent.com/pod-product-compliance
Lightning Source LLC
LaVergne TN
LVHW072018060526
838200LV00060B/4696